The
Talking
Tabby Cat

A FOLK TALE FROM FRANCE

retold by Jane Belk Moncure
illustrated by Helen Endres

ELGIN, ILLINOIS 60120

Original Folk Tale — "Puss in Boots"

Library of Congress Cataloging in Publication Data

Moncure, Jane Belk.
   The talking tabby cat.

   SUMMARY: A retelling of the tale of a cunning cat
who wins for her master the lordship of a manor and
the hand of a princess.
   [1. Fairy tales.   2. Folklore—France]   I. Endres,
Helen.   II. Puss in Boots.   III. Title.
PZ8.M753Tal   398.2'452'9744280944   [E]   79-26193
ISBN 0-89565-107-6

Distributed by Childrens Press, 1224 West Van Buren Street,
Chicago, Illinois 60607.

The
Talking
Tabby Cat

There was once an old miller who had three sons. To the oldest son, he gave his mill. To the second son, he gave his donkey. To the youngest son, he gave all that he had left in the world—a little tabby cat.

Now the tabby cat was the only possession the youngest son had. He looked at the little cat in sorrow.

"What will become of us?" he said to himself. "How will we eat? Where will we live?"

"Kind master," said the tabby cat, "do not worry. Dress me in fine clothes and a pair of boots. Then fetch me a basket. I will help you."

"A talking cat!" said the miller's son. He was so surprised that he did exactly as the cat had asked.

When the little tabby cat was dressed, she said, "Your kindness will be greatly rewarded, good master."

Then Tabby took her basket to a nearby
hen house. After filling the basket with fresh
eggs, she skipped across the fields to the
palace to see the king.

"Good morning, Your Majesty," she said. "I have brought you a gift from my good master, the Marquis of Carrabas."

The king was surprised by this remarkable talking tabby cat! In fact, he could hardly believe his ears. So he took the gifts and said, "Tell your master I am most grateful for this kindness."

The next day, Tabby found an orchard. She picked a basket of ripe, red apples. She took them to the king. This time, she saw the king's beautiful daughter.

"And your master is the Marquis of Carrabas?" the princess asked. "Tell him he has the best tasting apples in the kingdom!"

Then the princess took Tabby to the royal kitchen. There she poured a bowl of sweet cream for the little cat.

Shortly after that, Tabby heard that the king and his daughter were going for a carriage ride along the river. She ran to her master.

"Good Master, I have a plan that will bring you great happiness. First, you must jump into the river and make a big splash. Then, when the king asks your name, you must tell him you are the Marquis of Carrabas."

"But I am not a marquis. A marquis is rich and owns much land. And where is this Carrabas anyway?"

"It doesn't matter where Carrabas is. And truly, before this day ends, you will be a marquis," said Tabby. "Now jump!"

At that, the miller's son jumped into the swift river and splashed about.

When the king's royal carriage appeared, Tabby cried, "Help! Help! My good master, the Marquis of Carrabas, has fallen into the river! Help him!"

The king stopped the carriage at once. He sent three nobles to pull the young man out of the river.

And there the young man stood, his clothes muddy, soggy, and dripping.

"Your Majesty," said Tabby, "my master has no dry clothes to wear."

"We cannot leave the marquis here without dry clothing," said the princess.

"Certainly not!" said the king. He sent a guard back to the palace for one of his own royal suits.

Soon the miller's son was dressed in the beautiful garment. My, he looked grand! He looked so fine that the king invited him to join them for the rest of their ride.

"Sit beside me," said the princess. "Tell me about your remarkable talking tabby cat."

While this was happening, Tabby hurried up the road ahead of the carriage. Soon she came to the orchard where she had picked the basket of apples. Two men were working there.

"Tell me, kind sirs," she said, "who owns this orchard?"

"The terrible ogre," they replied. "He lives in yon castle. He owns this orchard and all these lands." They trembled, for they were much afraid of the ogre.

"From this day on," said Tabby, "all these lands belong to the Marquis of Carrabas. Tell the king just that when he rides by."

The men promised to do it. After all, they didn't like the ogre. And they had never before heard of a talking tabby cat.

Soon the king's carriage reached the orchard.

"Oh, look, Father," said the princess. "Ripe, red apples! This must be where those lovely apples that Tabby brought us were grown!"

"You there," the king called out the window. "Who owns this orchard?"

"The Marquis of Carrabas," the men answered, bowing low. "He owns the orchard and all these lands."

Once more, Tabby hurried ahead. Reaching the ogre's castle, she knocked on the door.

"Good day," she said to the ogre. "I have come from far away to see your magic."

The cruel ogre could hardly believe his ears—a cat who could talk! "What would you like to see?" he asked, and invited her into his castle.

J.P. OGRE
ESQ

NO
PEDDLERS

NO
LOITERING

"I have heard that you can turn yourself into any animal you choose," she said.

"Yes, I can!" said the ogre. "I can do anything!" At that, he turned himself into a lion.

"Oh, my!" said Tabby as she climbed up on a book shelf.

"Ha, ha!" roared the ogre. "I can be bigger yet!" And he turned himself into a huge elephant. Tabby scrambled to the very top of the shelves.

MOTHER SPOOK

WHOS WHO OF OGRES

FAMOUS BAD GUYS

PUBLIC SPOOKING

GHOUL FRIENDS

POTIONS + NOTIONS

ANYTHING GHOST

MAGIC TRICKS

DR. SPOOK

Whos afraid of

CO. SCHOOLS

C881316

25

"That is indeed a fine trick!" said Tabby. "But you were very large to start with. Can you do a harder trick? Can you turn into a tiny animal? Like a mouse?"

"Oh, of course!" said the ogre. And suddenly, he became a tiny, tiny mouse.

poof!

That was exactly what Tabby was waiting for! With one swift pounce, she put an end to the terrible ogre.

Soon the king's carriage came into sight. Tabby ran to greet the king.

"Welcome, Your Majesty," said Tabby, curtseying low. "Welcome, my princess. Welcome to the castle of my master, the Marquis of Carrabas."

The king turned to the miller's son. "In all my life, I have seen nothing so grand as your orchards and your fields. Now I see this grand castle!"

"Your Majesty," the young man replied, "in all my life, I have seen no one so beautiful as your daughter." He took the princess' hand in his own.

"That settles it," said the king. "I hereby declare you Prince of Carrabas!"

By this time, people were spreading the news. "The ogre is gone! The ogre is gone!" There was great joy! Soon the castle was filled with the sound of music.

The happy prince danced with the equally happy princess. That very night, the princess agreed to be his bride.

As for the talking tabby cat, there was a bowl of sweet cream for her every morning. She had a soft, silk pillow to sleep on each night. And from that day on, she was so happy that all she ever said was, "Purrrr!"